She Went From Dreaming to Doing

A Transformational Guide for The Woman Ready To Arise and Champion The Dream Within

LaToya Moulton

All glory belongs to God, who authors every dreamer's becoming.

This publication is a work of encouragement and inspiration. It is not intended as a substitute for professional advice, counseling, or therapy. It is sold with the understanding that the author and publisher is not engaged in giving psychological, legal, nor financial, or other professional advice. Please seek the help of a qualified professional if counseling is needed.

ISBN: 979-8-218-67098-6
Printed in the United States of America

Author's Note

To the courageous dreamer holding this book,
Thank you for saying yes to this journey.

She Went From Dreaming to Doing was born in the quiet moments between whispered prayers, journal pages filled with hope, and the tension of doubt and fear. It was written while I wrestled with insecurity, uncertainty, and the decision to keep going even when I couldn't see what was ahead. This devotional isn't just something I wrote. It's something I am living.

It was created on the edge between healing and becoming. In seasons where I felt unseen yet kept showing up anyway. In moments when I questioned my worth but chose to believe there was more for me. Through it all, one truth continued to ground me:

"For I know the plans I have for you, declares the Lord,
plans to prosper you and not to harm you,
plans to give you hope and a future."
Jeremiah 29:11

This scripture has been one of my anchor promises, but its roots run deep. I first encountered it during a transitional season in my life—fresh out of high school, standing at the crossroads of becoming. I carried a dream to become a writer, and utilize my voice in public speaking. The desire was strong, but the path forward felt unclear.

Author's Note

Around that same time, I experienced one of my earliest wounds to my sense of calling and direction. Someone I admired and trusted spoke words that not only belittled my gift but attempted muffle my voice. I remember leaving that conversation questioning everything about myself and the very dream God had placed inside me. Because those words were wrapped in religious language, "love", and presented as spiritual truth part of me believed they had to be right. Negative words spoken have a way of lingering. When we don't take the time to truly investigate it under the *light of truth*. Looking back now I know two things to be true. First, "they" were wrong and second the projections of another person's failed attempts, unresolved trauma, pain, fear, and lived experiences does not make it my truth.

But trauma has a way of distorting your vision. It makes you settle for crumbs when God has already prepared a seat for you at the table. I carried that echo of a lie for very long time. Until one day, overwhelmed and unsure, I whispered a raw prayer through tears:

"God, I know what I think about me, and those thoughts aren't always good. I know what others think about me. But I need to know... what do You think about me?"

It was time I had to confront the lie. In my bedroom on my knees. My tears became my prayer. I reached for my Bible, and without knowing where to turn, I opened it.

Author's Note

Out of sixty six books, it opened to Jeremiah. Out of all the chapters in Jeremiah, the pages of my bible fell open to chapter 29. And as I sat there heard I this gentle whisper "Look down." and my eyes landed and locked in on verse 11.

" For I know the thoughts I think toward you said the LORD, thoughts of peace...." Jeremiah 29:11

Here the Creator of the Universe stepped down into my personal affairs in that very moment to answer me. That moment marked the beginning of my personal invitation to dream with God. Not just to believe He had plans—but to trust that His plans were good, personal, and intentional. Since then, this verse has been a lifeline. A reminder that the God who holds all things together also sees me. He knows my longings. He is not intimidated by my questions or unaware of my struggles. He designed me with purpose and calls me by name.

My journey with Him has been one of trust, stumble, get back up, fall again, trust Him some more—to believe that even when the path doesn't look like what I imagined, His purpose is still unfolding beautifully. Before you turn the page, I want you to know this: What you're holding is more than a book. It is a compass. A guidepost. A reminder that your walk with God is a journey one filled with lessons, markers, turns, and holy pauses. The imagery throughout these pages is intentional. God is leading you somewhere.

Author's Note

She Went From Dreaming to Doing is an invitation to pick that dream back up from the shelf of life. To step out of comfort and complacency. To run your race with your eyes fixed on Him, the One who calls you forward is faithful to see you through.

This journey is a marathon, not a sprint. There is no need for comparison or competition. Nothing about God is scarce. His resources are limitless, His provision abundant, and His faithfulness unwavering. Will it be easy? No. Will there be challenges? Yes. Will there be moments when you want to quit? Absolutely. But will God meet you, strengthen you, and restore you? Without question.

You are not reading this by accident. From the beginning, God has prepared good works for you to walk in. And today, I stand not as a victim of my story—but as a victorious one who has been redeemed, carried, and strengthened by the grace of God.

And now, my sister, I speak this over you: It is time to arise and champion your dream. You do not have to be perfect to begin. You only have to be willing. This is only the beginning. And I am so proud of you for taking the first step.

With love,
LaToya
Your sister in faith, purpose, and daring to dream courageously

Before The Doing: A Reminder of Your Significance

Before we move forward, I want to anchor you in something deeper than strategy or goals—identity. You are not just a dreamer. You are a daughter.

A beloved, redeemed, seen, and cherished daughter of a loving Father. The doing. The dreaming. The rising.

All of it flows from this place. Not from pressure. Not from proving. Not from perfection. Not from performance. But from being deeply rooted in the love of God and who He has created you to be. She went from dreaming to doing when she realized that her action wasn't about earning love—it was an expression of it. Her obedience, creativity, and courage flowed from knowing she was already loved, already chosen, already held.

As you embark on this journey, you are not called to prove yourself or perform for approval. God is not asking you to become someone else. He is inviting you to trust what He has already placed within you—and to show up from that place of security and faith.

Before you do anything, remember this:
You are already enough.
You are already loved.
And you are already held.

How to Champion Your Dream

To champion your dream means you choose to stand with it—especially when it feels fragile, unfinished, or unseen.

It's deciding that your dream is worth protecting, nurturing, and believing in, even before others understand it. Championing your dream doesn't mean you have all the answers. It means you are willing to take responsibility for what God has entrusted to you.

You champion your dream when you stop waiting for permission and start honoring the quiet conviction within your heart. When you speak life instead of doubt. When you take small, faithful steps instead of waiting for perfect clarity.

Championing your dream also means learning how to tend to it with care. You guard it from voices that diminish it. You give it room to grow at its own pace. And you remain committed even when progress feels slow. This doesn't require striving or pressure. It requires trust, courage, and consistency. God is not asking you to force what He is growing. He's inviting you to partner with Him—one step at a time.

When you champion your dream, you're not just pursuing a goal. You're honoring obedience. You're choosing alignment.
You're saying yes to becoming. You're saying yes to
Co-Creating with God. And that decision
changes everything.

How to Let Go

Letting go isn't about giving up—it's about making room. Room for peace. Room for healing. Room for the new thing God wants to do in your life.

To let go means releasing what no longer serves you:

- Old narratives that say you're not enough
- Fear that disguises itself as control
- Bitterness, guilt, and shame that quietly weigh you down

Letting go is a holy surrender. It's the quiet decision to say, "God, I trust You more than I trust my own grip."

This release doesn't always happen all at once. Often, it's a process. But every time you loosen your hold on what has been weighing you down, you rise a little higher. With each step, you create space to breathe, heal, and move forward with greater freedom.

Letting go may look like this:

- Choosing to get back up after a fall
- Releasing who you had to be to survive and daring to become who you were created to be

How to Let Go

- Getting curious and allowing yourself to question the labels and limitations placed on you—by culture, family patterns, religious language, or the unresolved fears of others
- Sitting with honest questions like: Who told me I couldn't? Where did this belief begin? Why am I afraid to try? Why do I feel like it has to be perfect?

Letting go is both spiritual and practical. It's a posture of the heart and a choice of the will. This kind of inner work requires moments of slowing down, rest, and stillness.

In these moments, trust the One who knows you fully and holds every detail of your life with care. God brings hidden wounds into the light—not to shame you, but to heal what has been damaged and restore what has been taken. Freedom begins when truth is revealed.

And here is the beautiful truth:

You don't have to rise perfectly.
You just have to trust—and rise.

How to Trust God and Believe in Your God-Given Capabilities

Trusting God is more than words—it's an active decision to lean not on your own understanding. It's learning to rest in what you cannot yet see and believing that the One who called you is also the One who will equip you and see you through.

But trust isn't only about God's ability—it's also about your agreement. You have to believe that He placed something valuable inside you. Yes, you. With all your questions, flaws, and history. To trust God and believe in your God-given capabilities means remembering:

- Who He is
- What He has already brought you through
- That He does not make mistakes—and that includes you

Trust invites partnership. God supplies the grace, direction, and strength, but you bring your willingness. Your yes matters. Your obedience matters. Your belief matters. So hear this clearly:

You are not behind.
You are not disqualified.
You are not too late.

You are chosen.
You are gifted.
You are ready.
And you are next.

The Power of Community: Finding Your 3 C's

You were never meant to walk this journey alone.

Healing, growth, and bold action flourish in the soil of safe, healthy community. God often uses people to strengthen us, steady us, and remind us of who we are when the road feels long.

As you step into this ninety-day journey, pause and ask yourself: Who is walking with me?

You need people who don't just see you—but champion you.

Look for the 3 C's:

- Challenge You
- Friends who won't let you play small. Who lovingly call you higher, remind you of your identity, and encourage you to rise when you forget your strength.
- Cover You in Prayer
- Sisters who intercede for you behind the scenes. Who lift your name in prayer and speak God's truth over your life when you feel weary or uncertain.
- Celebrate You
- People who rejoice with you in the wins, sit with you in the losses, and remind you that you are worth celebrating—not just for what you do, but for who you are.

The Power of Community: Finding Your 3 C's

This journey is sacred and deeply personal—and yes, at times it may feel lonely. But the right community will remind you of this truth:

You don't have to do it all alone.
You just have to keep showing up with the right people beside you.

So take a moment. Pray for alignment. Open your heart to the people God is sending.

Your 3 C's may be the very thing that helps you keep going—
the difference between quitting and rising

Before You Begin

As you step into Day 1, you'll begin to see this devotional as more than pages. It's a map for your journey.

Each affirmation, each coachable moment, and each reflection serves as a marker along the path God is guiding you through.

Some days will feel like clear, open roads.
Others may feel like gentle turns—inviting you to slow down and look within.

Before You Begin

Throughout this devotional, you'll encounter moments marked as Holy Pause. These are intentional spaces for reflection, rest, and listening. They are not meant to rush you forward, but to invite you deeper. In these moments, you're encouraged to slow down, revisit what God has been stirring in you, and simply be present. There is no pressure to move quickly—growth happens in both motion and stillness.

You'll begin to notice how every step, even the small ones, is moving you forward.

Let God be your compass.
Let His voice steady your pace and direct your heart.

These ninety days are not meant to rush you.
They are meant to walk with you, strengthen you, and help you recognize the ways He has been leading you all along.

So take your time.
Breathe.

You are not wandering.
You are being led.

And I am cheering you on with every step you take.

DAY 1

Answering the Call

Affirmation: *I am ready to answer the call of my dream with faith and action.*

Coachable Moment:

A dream is more than just a passing thought, it's a call. A pull toward something greater. But answering that call requires courage. It requires saying yes before all the details make sense. It requires trusting that if God placed the dream within you, He has also given you the ability to achieve it.

The moment you say YES to your dream, you shift something in the atmosphere. You begin stepping into the person you are meant to be. Today is the day to start. Will you answer the call?

Journaling Prompt - Inner Reflection

What dream or purpose has been calling me?
What has been holding me back from answering?

....

....

....

....

....

....

....

....

....

....

....

....

Here I am. Send me. - Isaiah 6:8

DAY 2

Fear is Just a Feeling

Affirmation: *I take action despite fear because my dreams are bigger than my doubts.*

Coachable Moment:

Fear often disguises itself as logic. It whispers reasons why you should wait, why you're not ready, why now isn't the time. But the truth? Fear is just a feeling, not a fact.

The difference between those who achieve their dreams and those who don't has nothing to do with a lack of fear it's a refusal to let fear decide for them. Courage is not about waiting for fear to disappear when that feeling does show up. It's about stepping forward while fear is still trying to whisper.

Today, you get to decide: Will you let fear hold you back, or will you move forward anyway?

Journaling Prompt - Inner Reflection

What fear has been holding me back?
How can I choose to move forward in faith, and what's one small action?

For God has not given us a spirit of fear, but of power, love and a sound mind. - 2nd Timothy 1:7

DAY 3

Breaking the Chains of Doubt

Affirmation: *I release insecurity and embrace my confidence.*

Coachable Moment:

Doubt is a heavy weight to carry. It convinces you that you're not enough, not ready, not capable. But here's the truth: You have everything you need within you.

Every time you choose to believe in yourself, doubt loses its grip. Every time you take a step forward, you're proving that the voice of insecurity isn't telling the truth. You are worthy of success. You are capable of greatness. You belong in every room you step into.

Journaling Prompt - Inner Reflection

Where do I feel doubt creeping in?
What truth can I replace those doubts with today?

I sought the LORD, and he answered me; he delivered me from all my fears. - Psalm 34:4

DAY 4

Faith Over Fear

Affirmation: *I trust that every step God tells me to take is leading me toward my purpose. I can trust His leading.*

Coachable Moment:

Fear tells you to stop, but faith invites you to move forward. Fear whispers that you are not enough, not ready, not capable. Faith reminds you that you were created for this moment. Fear focuses on what could go wrong. Faith anchors you in what God has already promised.

Fear will always try to speak up when you are on the edge of growth. Those nagging thoughts. The quiet doubts. The familiar voice of your inner critic. They do not mean you are failing. They mean you are standing at a crossroads.

The real question is not whether fear will show up. It is which voice you will choose to follow.

Faith or fear?
Growth or comfort?
Progress or hesitation?
God's promises or the pressure to stay safe?

Journaling Prompt - Inner Reflection

Where in my life have I allowed fear to take the lead?
What would it look like to trust faith instead, even in the small ways?

When I am afraid, I put my trust in You. - Psalm 56:3

DAY 5

Small Steps, Big Impacts

Affirmation: *Progress, not perfection is my path to success.*

Coachable Moment:

Sometimes we convince ourselves that big dreams require big, dramatic moves. But real transformation rarely happens in one giant leap. It happens quietly, consistently, and one step at a time.

Think of a staircase. Every step matters. You don't reach the top by skipping the process. You climb by placing one foot in front of the other, trusting that each step is carrying you higher.

Progress doesn't always fell impressive. Often, it looks small. Ordinary. Easy to overlook. But those small, faithful steps are exactly how momentum is built.

Today, instead of focusing on how far you still have to go, bring your attention to the next right step. The one that's within reach. The one you can take right now. Small steps taken consistently, lead to lasting change.

Journaling Prompt - Inner Reflection

What has progress looked like for me recently, even if it didn't feel significant at the time?
How can I honor and celebrate my growth with waiting for perfection?

Do not despise these small beginnings, for the LORD rejoices to see the work begin. - Zechariah 4:10

DAY 6

Imposter Syndrome Has No Power

Affirmation: *I belong in every room I step into.*

Coachable Moment:

Have you ever walked into a room and suddenly felt like you didn't belong? Like everyone else knew something you didn't? That quiet voice questioning your presence, your ability, your worth? That's imposter syndrome talking.

Here's the truth: you are not here by accident.

Your voice, your talents, your skills, your presence, and your dreams were not randomly assigned. God created you for a purpose and your life has significance. You carry value simply because you exist, and you are meant to take up space. Today, I invite you to challenge the lie and step fully into the truth.

You are worthy.
You are capable.
You belong.

This is your time to rise.

Journaling Prompt - Inner Reflection

Where have I noticed imposter syndrome showing up in my thoughts or actions?
What truth can I remind myself of when doubt tries to take the lead?

....

....

....

....

....

....

....

....

....

....

....

You are God's workmanship, created in Christ Jesus to do good works. - Ephesians 2:10

DAY 7

Walking in Boldness

Affirmation: *My voice, ideas, and presence matter. I will not shrink myself.*

Coachable Moment:

Boldness isn't about being the loudest in the room it's about showing up fully as yourself, without apology.

Too often, we hold back. We play small. We wait for permission. We second guess our own brilliance. But you were not created to blend into the background. You were created to stand tall, take up space, and own your God-given gifts.

Walking in boldness means deciding who you are today is enough.
No more hiding. No more downplaying your strengths.
You are here for a reason own it.

Journaling Prompt - Inner Reflection

Where in my life have I been playing small?
How can I step into my power with apology?

....

....

....

....

....

....

....

....

....

....

....

The righteous are as bold as a lion. - Proverbs 28:1

DAY 8

I Was Created for This

Affirmation: *My purpose is already within me. I am fully equipped for my journey.*

Coachable Moment:

Sometimes we chase success as if it's something outside of us, something we have to earn or prove. But what if everything you need has already been placed within you?

God doesn't call the equipped. He equips the called. Every experience, every lesson, every challenge you've walked through has been preparing you for this very moment. Nothing has been wasted.

You were created with purpose, on purpose.

The dreams in your heart are not random. They are aligned with who you were created to be. You don't need to become someone else to live your calling. You simply need to trust what God has already placed inside you.

Journaling Prompt - Inner Reflection

What are three gifts, strengths, or experiences I already have that support my purpose?
How does it feel to fully embrace my calling without hesitstion or comparison?

....

....

....

....

....

....

....

....

....

....

....

Before I formed you in the womb I knew you. - Jeremiah 1:5

DAY 9

Overcoming the "What if's?"

Affirmation: *I choose faith over overthinking. I will not let "what if's" steal my focus and detour me from my destiny.*

Coachable Moment:

How many times have you talked yourself out of something because of a what if ?

What if I fail?
What if this doesn't work?
What if I'm not ready?

But what if you succeed? What if this opportunity changes your life? What if you are already enough? Overthinking creates obstacles that don't exist. The truth is, most of the things we fear never even happen.

The only thing standing between you and your next breakthrough is the courage to move forward despite uncertainty. Faith doesn't require all the answers. It only asks for your next step.

Journaling Prompt - Inner Reflection

How can I begin shifting my focus from limitations to possibilities today?

Trust in the LORD with all your heart and lean not
on your own understanding. - Proverbs 3:5

HOLY PAUSE

A Sacred Moment of Rest and Reflection

DAY 10

Coachable Moment: *The Call Begins*

Before Moses ever led a people, he questioned himself.

When God called him, Moses didn't respond with confidence or clarity. He responded with hesitation. Who am I to do this? Why would You choose me? What if I fail? He saw his limitations more clearly than his calling.

And yet, God didn't withdraw the invitation.

God didn't argue with Moses' insecurity or demand instant confidence. Instead, He met Moses with His presence. He reminded him that the call was never dependent on Moses' ability—it was anchored in God's faithfulness.

This Holy Pause is a reminder that doubt does not disqualify you. Questioning does not cancel the call. Often, the very place where you feel unsure is where God first introduces Himself more deeply.

If you are standing at the edge of the unknown, wondering if you're capable, qualified, or ready—know this: God is not intimidated by your questions. He calls you anyway.

Journaling Prompt - Inner Reflection

How can I begin shifting my focus from limitations to possibilities today?

....

....

....

....

....

....

....

....

....

....

....

....

Now go; I will help you speak and will teach you what to say. - Exodus 4:12

DAY 11

From Overthinking to Action

Affirmation: *I refuse to stay tuck in my head. I choose action over hesitation.*

Coachable Moment:

Overthinking feels like progress, but it's really just fear in disguise. The more we analyze, the more we convince ourselves to wait, delay, and second-guess our God-given capabilities.

But clarity doesn't come from thinking it comes from doing. The fastest way to overcome doubt is to take action, even if it's messy.

Today, silence the endless thoughts and just start. Even one small step moves you forward and closer to your goals.

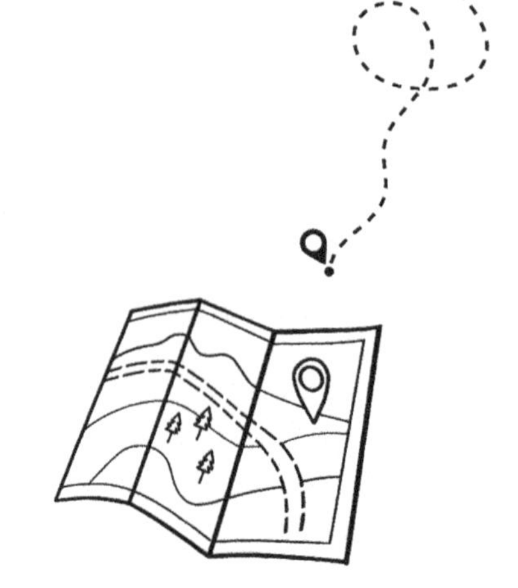

Journaling Prompt - Inner Reflection

What is something I've been overthinking?
What imperfect action can I take today that will move me forward?

Whatever you do, do it with all your heart, as working for the LORD. - Colossians 3:23

DAY 12

Confidence is a Muscle

Affirmation: *Every time I show up, I build confidence. I am growing stronger daily.*

Coachable Moment:

Confidence isn't something you're born with it's something you build. Like a muscle, the more you use it, the stronger it gets.

Every time you speak up, take a risk, or believe in yourself, you're strengthening that confidence muscle.

You don't have to feel 100% ready to take action. You just have to be willing. And the more you do, the easier it becomes.

Journaling Prompt - Inner Reflection

What is one moment you felt confident in yourself?
How can you continue to build confidence every day?

Do not throw away your confidence; it will be richly rewarded. - Hebrews 10:35

DAY 13

No More Playing Small

Affirmation: *I step fully into my calling. I refuse to shrink myself for the comfort of others.*

Coachable Moment:

For too long, you've dimmed your light. You've held back your ideas, downplayed your wins, and made yourself smaller to avoid making others uncomfortable.

But the world doesn't need a muted version of you.

It needs you fully alive, fully present, and fully YOU. You were not given a dream just to tuck it away or keep it hidden. What God placed inside you was meant to be seen, shared, and stewarded

No more shrinking. No more apologizing. You are here to take up space, to shine, and to lead.

Journaling Prompt - Inner Reflection

Where in my life have I been playing small?
How would my life change if I showed up a little more fully as myself?

Arise shine, for your light has come. - Isaiah 60:1

DAY 14

Fear Does Not Define Me

Affirmation: *I am more than my emotions. Fear may rise, but it does not rule me. My purpose is permanent.*

Coachable Moment:

Fear is a feeling, not a fact.

It's your mind's way of trying to keep you safe. And sometimes, that protection is necessary. But other times, fear doesn't mean danger — it means growth. It signals that you're standing at the edge of something unfamiliar, something that requires trust, courage, and movement.

When left unexamined, fear can keep you too safe. It can protect you from failure, yes — but it can also protect you from growth, progress, and the fullness of the life God designed you to live.

Fear is not something to ignore or shame. It's something to investigate.

Today, remind yourself: I can feel fear and still move forward. I am not defined by my doubts. I am defined by my faith, my resilience, and my willingness to trust God beyond what feels comfortable.

Journaling Prompt - Inner Reflection

What fear has been showing up in my life, and what might it be trying to tell me?

Perfect love casts out fear. - 1 John 4:18

DAY 15

I Am Becoming

Affirmation: *Every day, I am evolving into the highest version of myself.*

Coachable Moment:

You don't have to have it all figured out to be on the right path. Growth isn't about being perfect it's about becoming.

Think about where you were one year ago. The version of you who was still figuring things out. The prayers you whispered. The fears you carried quietly. The steps you took even when you weren't sure they would work.

Now pause and notice you're still here. You've grown, learned, and changed in ways you couldn't have imagined back then.

The same will be true a year from now.

So trust the process. Celebrate your progress.
And remind yourself that becoming is not something you rush – it's something you honor.

Journaling Prompt - Inner Reflection

What is one way I can see evidence of my growth over the past year?

He who began a good work in you will carry it on to completion. - Philippians 1:6

DAY 16

God Goes Before Me

Affirmation: *I am covered by God. I am never alone, my steps are ordered.*

Coachable Moment:

Sometimes, the weight of figuring it all out can feel overwhelming. But here's the good news: It's not a requirement to have everything figured out before you proceed to trust and the bonus you don't have to do this alone.

God has already gone before you, clearing paths, aligning opportunities, and making ways you haven't even seen yet.

Today, release the need to carry it all. Trust that you are guided, protected, and exactly where you're meant to be.

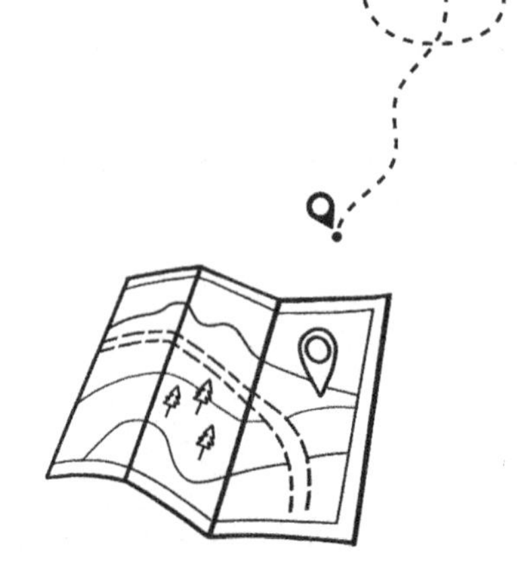

Journaling Prompt - Inner Reflection

How can I let go of control and embrace God's divine timing?

The Lord himself goes before you and will be with you. - Deuteronomy 31:8

DAY 17

I Am Worthy of Good Things

Affirmation: *I release guilt and embrace the blessings meant for me..*

Coachable Moment:

Have you ever found yourself feeling guilty for wanting more? More joy, more peace, more success? Maybe you've been conditioned to settle to believe that wanting more makes you ungrateful.

But God delights in blessing you. You are not meant to just survive you are meant to thrive.

Today, give yourself permission to receive every blessing coming your way.

Journaling Prompt - Inner Reflection

What limiting beliefs have made me feel guilty about success, joy, or abundance? How can I open my heart to receive all the good God has for me without guilt?

....

....

....

....

....

....

....

....

....

....

....

....

No good thing does He withhold from those who walk uprightly. - Psalm 84:11

DAY 18

Walking in Alignment

Affirmation: *I trust God's divine timing and know that I am exactly where I need to be.*

Coachable Moment:

There is nothing more exhausting than chasing things that are not meant for you.

But alignment doesn't always look like ease. Sometimes it looks like clarity. Sometimes it looks like conviction. And sometimes it looks like resistance that strengthens you rather than stops you.

When you're out of alignment, everything feels heavy, forced, and draining. When you're in alignment, even the hard things carry purpose. You may still have to push, stretch, and persevere — but there is peace beneath the effort. A knowing that you are moving in the right direction, even when it's not easy. Discernment is key.

Today reflect on where you feel clarity, not just comfort. Where your values, faith, and purpose are aligned - even if the road still requires courage. Those are the places you're meant to be. Trust God enough to stay there.

Journaling Prompt - Inner Reflection

Where in my life do I feel resistance that is refining me, versus resistance that is draining me?

In all your ways acknowledge Him, and He will make your paths straight. - Proverbs 3:6

DAY 19

Courage is a Choice

Affirmation: *Every day I choose to be brave, even in small ways.*

Coachable Moment:

Courage isn't the absence of fear it's the decision to move forward anyway.

Some days, courage looks like taking a leap of faith. Other days, it looks like getting out of bed, showing up, and trying again.

Big or small, every act of courage counts. Today, choose bravery in whatever way you can.

Journaling Prompt - Inner Reflection

What are three small acts of courage I can take today? How can I remind myself that courage is a daily choice?

Have I not commanded you? Be strong and courageous.
Do not be afraid; do not be discouraged, for the LORD
your God will be with you. - Joshua 1:9

HOLY PAUSE

A Sacred Moment of Rest and Reflection

DAY 20

Coachable Moment: *You Are the Champion of Your Dream*

No one else can run your race for you.

Others may cheer you on. Some may doubt you. A few may never understand the path you're walking. But the responsibility and the privilege of stewarding your dream belongs to you. Being the champion of your dream doesn't mean you never feel fear. It means you don't let fear make your decisions.

It means you show up even when motivation fades, choosing consistency over comfort and faith over excuses. God entrusted this dream to you on purpose. Not because you were perfect or fully prepared, but because you were willing. Willing to grow, learn, and rise after every setback.

Today is a reminder: you are not waiting to be chosen. You already are. Now it's time to stand, move forward, and champion what has been placed in your hands.

Journaling Prompt - Inner Reflection

What dream am I being called to take full ownership of in this season? What does championing my dream look like in my daily choices, starting today?

He makes my feet like the feet of a deer, And sets me on my high places. - Psalm 18:33

DAY 21

Failure is Not an Option

Affirmation: *I am determined, resilient, and unstoppable.*

Coachable Moment:

When you shift your perspective and take failure off the table, something shifts. You stop seeing obstacles as roadblocks and start seeing them as lessons.

Every setback is a setup for a comeback. Every challenge is a chance to grow. You will not quit. You will pivot, learn, and keep moving forward.

Your dream is worth the fight. Keep going.

Journaling Prompt - Inner Reflection

How can I reframe failure as a lesson instead of a loss?
What is one challenge I've overcome that made me stronger?

He makes my feet like the feet of a deer, And sets me on my high places. - Psalm 18:33

DAY 22

I Am Stronger Than I Think

Affirmation: *I trust my inner strength and ability to overcome any challenge.*

Coachable Moment:

You've survived every hard day, every setback, and every storm that was meant to break you. Somehow your still standing.

That alone tells a powerful story.

Strength doesn't always look like confidence or certainty. Sometimes strength looks like taking one more step when quitting would feel easier. Choosing hope when fear is loud. And sometimes, strength looks like knowing when to rest.

When doubt creeps in, remind yourself of this truth: God has already carried you through so much. The same grace that sustained you then is still holding you now.
You will get through this too.

Journaling Prompt - Inner Reflection

When was a time I surprised myself with my own strength and resilience? How can I remind myself today that God's grace is sufficient for me?

But He said to me, My grace is sufficient for you, for my power is made perfect in weakness. - 2nd Corinthians 12:9

DAY 23

Prayer Is My Power

Affirmation: *I pray boldly, trusting that God hears me, leads me, and goes before me.*

Coachable Moment:

Prayer is not a last resort.
It's your first line of strength.

Prayer is where dreams are clarified, fear is quieted, and direction becomes clear. It's where you stop carrying everything alone and invite God into the process — not just the outcome.

Prayer doesn't mean you sit back and wait. It means you move forward with confidence, knowing you're not moving by yourself.

Some prayers don't change your circumstances right away, but they always change you. They align your heart, sharpen your discernment, and remind you who is truly in control.

Today, don't underestimate the power of a simple, honest prayer. God is not intimidated by your questions, your doubts, or your dreams.
Bring it all to Him — and then walk forward in faith.

Journaling Prompt - Inner Reflection

What am I currently carrying that I need to release to God in prayer?
How can I cultivate prayer as a daily source of strength?

I call on you, my God, for you will answer me: turn your ear to me and hear my prayer. - Psalm 17:6

DAY 24

Permission to Succeed

Affirmation: *I give myself full permission to win.*

Coachable Moment:

Have you ever felt like you needed permission to go after your dreams? Like you were waiting for someone to validate your path?

Here's the truth: You don't need anyone's approval to walk in your calling.

God has already given you permission to succeed, to grow, to elevate, to shine fourth His light and inspire others. The only person who needs to say YES is you.

Journaling Prompt - Inner Reflection

Where in my life have, I been waiting for permission?
How can I start moving forward without waiting?

....

....

....

....

....

....

....

....

....

....

....

....

But now, this is what the LORD says - He who created you, He who formed you. Do not fear, for I have redeemed you: I have called you by name; you are Mine - Isaiah 43:1

DAY 25

Unshakable Faith

Affirmation: *I move forward, trusting the journey even when I can't see the full picture.*

Coachable Moment:

Faith is easy when things are going well but what about when things feel uncertain, delayed, or out of your control?

That's when real faith is tested. The kind that says, even though I don't see it yet, I trust that all things are working out for my good.

Today, choose to believe in the things that haven't manifested yet. Trust that every closed door, what may appear to be a delay, and every redirection is still part of God's ultimate plan for your life.

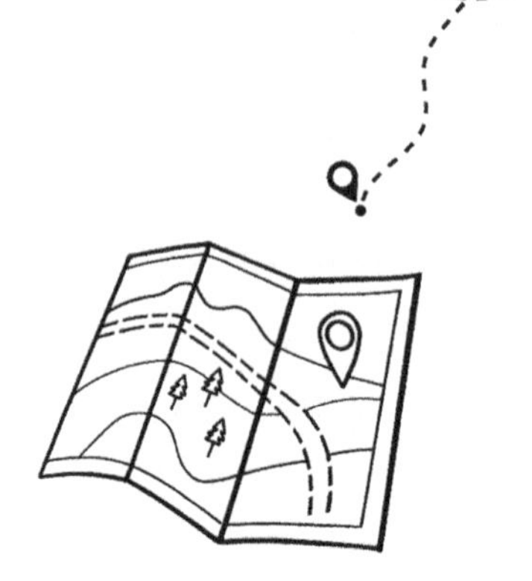

Journaling Prompt - Inner Reflection

Where am I struggling to trust God in the process?
How can I remind myself that what's for me won't miss me?

....

....

....

....

....

....

....

....

....

....

....

....

And we know that God causes all things to work together for good to those who love God,
to those who are called according to His purpose. - Romans 8:28

DAY 26

The Future is Calling

Affirmation: *I answer my calling with boldness and faith,*

Coachable Moment:

Your future self is watching. She's waiting for you to take the next step. She's already walking in the dreams you're afraid to step out and pursue.

What will you say when she asks, "Did you answer the call?"

This is your moment. Step forward. Say YES to the future that's waiting for you.

Journaling Prompt - Inner Reflection

How can I commit to answering the call?
What is one bold step I can take toward my future self today?

Speak LORD for your servant is listening. - 1st Samuel 3:9

DAY 27

Dreams Are Meant to Be Lived

Affirmation: *I take intentional action today to bring my dreams to life.*

Coachable Moment:

Dreams are not meant to sit in journals or vision boards. They are meant to be lived out one faithful step at a time.

Waiting for the perfect moment can quietly keep you stuck. The truth is, the perfect moment is rarely obvious. It's created through action. Through obedience. Through choosing to move even when you don't feel fully ready.

You don't need a full plan to begin. You need a willing heart and courage to take the next step placed in front of you.

One action.
One step.
One decision to move forward.

Journaling Prompt - Inner Reflection

What would it look like for me to turn my vision into intentional movement, even in small ways?

Anyone who listens to my teaching and follows it is wise, like a person who builds a house on a solid rock. - Proverbs 29:18

DAY 28

I Trust Myself

Affirmation: *I make decisions with confidence and clarity.*

Coachable Moment:

You've spent so much time second-guessing yourself, waiting for external validation, or overanalyzing every decision.

But the truth is you already know.

God has placed wisdom within you. And if you lack wisdom, ask Him for it. He's faithful to answer. Trust that. Trust yourself. The next step will reveal itself when you decide to move forward.

Journaling Prompt - Inner Reflection

Where in my life do I need to cultivate more trust?
What's one thing I can ask God for wisdom starting today?

Now if any of you lacks wisdom, he should ask God, who gives generously to all without finding fault, and it will be given to you. - James 1:5

DAY 29

Part of a Greater Plan

Affirmation: *My purpose and dreams are part of God's grand plan, and I trust His timing and design.*

Coachable Moment:

Your dream is not random.
Your purpose is not an afterthought.
It is woven into a story far greater than you can see right now.

God doesn't waste experiences, seasons, or desires. The dream stirring in your heart is connected to His plan, not separate from it. Even the delays, detours, and moments of uncertainty are shaping you for what's ahead.

You may not see how all the pieces fit together yet, but that doesn't mean they don't belong. God is working behind the scenes, aligning moments, people, and opportunities in ways only He can.

Today, release the pressure to figure it all out. Your role is not to control the plan. Your role is to trust, obey, and keep moving forward in faith.

What you're carrying has a place in God's bigger story.

Journaling Prompt - Inner Reflection

Where have I seen God's hand at work in my life?
How does it feel to trust that my dream is part of something greater than me?

....

....

....

....

....

....

....

....

....

....

....

....

Now For we are God's masterpiece. He has created us anew in Christ Jesus,
so we can do the things He planned for us long ago. - Ephesians 2:10

HOLY PAUSE

A Sacred Moment of Rest and Reflection

DAY 30

Coachable Moment: *Lies, Label's and Limitations*

Gideon saw himself as the least in his family, hiding in fear, threshing wheat in secret. His environment, his past, and his circumstances had shaped how he viewed himself. But God's perspective was entirely different.

When God called Gideon, He didn't address him by his fear or his insecurity. God called him mighty warrior. Before Gideon ever lifted a sword, before he ever led an army, God named him according to his true identity and purpose.

Like Gideon, maybe you've been living beneath the weight of lies you've believed, labels others placed on you, and limitations you may have accepted as truth. Perhaps you've allowed past experiences, criticism, and comparison to distort your vision of who you really are.

But today marks a divine interruption.
May God awakening your spiritual
sight even greater and cause you to see
who He has called you to be!
A Mighty Woman of Valor.

Journaling Prompt - Inner Reflection

What lies, labels, or limitations have shaped how I see myself?
If I fully believed who God says I am, how would I show up differently?

The LORD turned to him and said, Go in the strength you have..
Am I not sending you? - Judges 6:14

DAY 31

Renewing Your Mind

Affirmation: *I renew my mind daily with God's promises. I think in alignment with who I am becoming.*

Coachable Moment:

Spiritual growth doesn't begin with changing your circumstances—it begins with changing your thinking.

God may call you mighty, chosen, and equipped, but if your mind is still rehearsing old narratives, fear will try to reclaim its seat. That's why renewing your mind is not a one-time moment; it's a daily practice.

Every day, you are choosing which voice gets authority in your life. The voice of doubt? The voice of past experiences? Or the voice of truth?

Renewing your mind means intentionally replacing lies with truth. It means catching the thoughts that shrink you and challenging them with what God has already spoken over you. It's learning to pause, redirect, and align your thoughts with faith instead of fear.

Confidence rooted in God isn't loud or arrogant—it's steady. It's the quiet assurance that says, Even when I feel unsure, I am anchored.

Journaling Prompt - Inner Reflection

What recurring thought patterns do I need to surrender and renew?

Do not conform to the pattern of this world, but be transformed
by the renewing of your mind. - Romans 8:12

DAY 32

You Have to Speak Life

Affirmation: *I choose words that align with truth, faith, and the future God is forming in me.*

Coachable Moment:

Words carry power.

The words you speak shape the atmosphere around you and the beliefs within you. Long before actions change, language does. What you repeatedly say has a way of becoming what you eventually believe.

It's easy to speak from frustration, fear, or exhaustion. But speaking life requires intention. It means choosing words that reflect faith instead of finality, hope instead of limitation.

This doesn't mean ignoring reality or pretending things are perfect. It means refusing to let negative words define your future. Even in uncertain moments, your words can point toward growth, healing, and possibility.

Today, pay attention to how you speak about yourself. Choose to speak life.

Journaling Prompt - Inner Reflection

What words do I tend to speak over myself when I feel discouraged or tired? How can I intentionally speak life over my dreams, my identity, and my future today?

The tongue has the power of life and death, and those who love it will eat its fruit. - Proverbs 18:21

DAY 33

Standing Firm

Affirmation: *I stand firm in who God has called me to be.*
I walk in spiritual authority, grounded in truth.

Coachable Moment:

Spiritual authority isn't about volume, control, or dominance. It's about alignment.

When you know who you are and whose you are, you don't have to explain yourself or shrink back. You stand firm. Rooted. Steady. Unmoved by every opinion, obstacle, or opposition that comes your way.

Standing firm doesn't mean life won't challenge you. It means you've decided not to be shaken by what tries to intimidate or distract you. It's choosing to hold your ground in truth, even when pressure rises.

Spiritual authority grows when you consistently choose faith over fear, obedience over comfort, and trust over doubt. It's developed through surrender, prayer, and daily decisions to walk in alignment with God's Word.

Journaling Prompt - Inner Reflection

Where in my life is God asking me to stand firm instead of retreat or second-guess myself?

Be on your guard; stand firm in the faith; be courageous; be strong. - 1st Corinthians 16:13

DAY 34

Keep Going

Affirmation: *I remain faithful and persistent even when the journey seems long.*

Coachable Moment:

Perseverance isn't about pushing harder every day. Sometimes, it's about choosing not to quit.

There will be seasons when progress feels slow, when results aren't visible, and when the excitement that once fueled you begins to fade. These are the moments that quietly shape you.

Endurance is built in the ordinary. In the days you show up without applause. In the times you keep moving forward even when motivation runs low. God does some of His deepest work in these in-between seasons.

You don't need to rush this process. You don't need to prove anything. You only need to stay faithful to the step you're on.

Journaling Prompt - Inner Reflection

What would it look like for me to practice endurance with grace instead of pressure?

Let's us run with perseverance the race marked out for us . - Hebrews 12:1

DAY 35

How to Steward Your Dream

Affirmation: *I steward my dream with faith, wisdom and intention.*

Coachable Moment:

A dream is not just something to pursue.
It's something to steward.

When God places a dream in your heart, He entrusts you with responsibility — not pressure, but purpose. Stewardship means caring for what you've been given with intention, humility, and obedience.

Stewarding your dream looks like showing up when progress feels slow.
It looks like preparing in quiet seasons when no one is watching.
It means protecting your dream from comparison, rushing,
and unnecessary noise. Not every voice deserves access.
Not every season calls for the same pace.

Today, remember this: God is not asking you to force the dream into existence. He's asking you to walk with Him as it unfolds. When you steward your dream well, you create space for growth, clarity, and divine alignment.

Journaling Prompt - Inner Reflection

What does stewarding my dream look like in this current season of my life?

Whoever can be trusted with very little can also be trusted with much . - Luke 16:10

DAY 36

Stay the Course

Affirmation: *I will not give up. Even when it's hard, I keep going.*

Coachable Moment:

Resilience is often built in the trenches not on the mountaintop. Staying the course, doesn't mean ignoring rest or wisdom. It means remaining faithful to the path God has set before you, even when momentum slows.

Some seasons will test your patience more than your strength. Others will stretch your faith when results aren't immediate. But your consistency in the small, unseen moments is shaping you for greater impact

Stay the course. What you're building matters even when progress feels quiet.

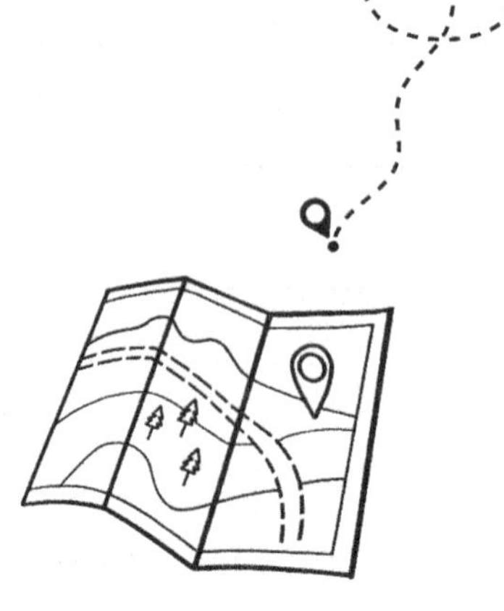

Journaling Prompt - Inner Reflection

What ways can I take care of myself during times of discouragement?

Go and enjoy choice food and sweet drinks, and send some to those who have nothing prepared. This day is holy to our Lord. Do not grieve, for the joy of the LORD is your strength . - Nehemiah 8:10

DAY 37

Perfection Is Not My Ally

Affirmation: *Every step I take matters. I release perfection and embrace progress.*

Coachable Moment:

Perfectionism is a relentless dream killer that hinders your progress. Remember, you don't need to achieve perfection; you simply need to keep moving forward. With every step, progress compounds and builds upon itself.

Trust in the pace that aligns with your life's journey, and let go of the need for flawlessness. Embrace your unique steady pace toward your dreams.

Journaling Prompt - Inner Reflection

Where are you holding yourself to a perfect standard and its slowing down your progress?

And you will know the truth, and the truth will set you free . - John 8:32

DAY 38

You Are Not Behind

Affirmation: *I am exactly where I need to be for my growth and purpose.*

Coachable Moment:

In today's quiet moment of reflection, let it become crystal clear: comparison is a thief of the soul's peace. Trust in God's perfect timing, uniquely designed for your life. You are not lagging behind; rather, you are being lovingly prepared for what lies ahead.

Embrace the now and find comfort in knowing that the divine storyline of your journey is still unfolding, guided by His hand as you trust Him.

Journaling Prompt - Inner Reflection

Where have I been tempted to compare my journey?
How can I create space right now to honestly pour out my heart to God?

The LORD is my shepherd, I lack nothing. He makes me lie down in green pastures,
He leads me beside quiet waters, He refreshes my soul . - Psalm 23:1-3

DAY 39

I Am a Magnet for Divine Opportunities

Affirmation: *I attract the right doors, the right connections, and the right opportunities at the right time.*

Coachable Moment:

You don't have to chase what's meant for you. You attract what you are divinely aligned with.

When you move in confidence, operate in purpose, and show up fully, the right opportunities find you. It's not luck—it's God aligning you with what has already been predestined for you.

So stop stressing about how things will happen.
Focus on becoming the woman
who is ready when they do.

Journaling Prompt - Inner Reflection

What is one way I can prepare yourself today for the opportunities I desire?

Take delight in the LORD, and he will give you
the desires of your heart. - Psalm 37:4

HOLY PAUSE

A Sacred Moment of Rest and Reflection

DAY 40

Coachable Moment: *Courageous Alignment*

Before Abraham ever took a step, he made a decision.

God called him to leave what was familiar to step away from comfort, certainty, and what made sense—and promised to show him the way as he went. Abraham didn't receive a map. He received a word.

Courageous alignment begins with an inner yes.

It's the moment you decide, "I trust God more than I trust what I can see." Alignment doesn't mean you feel fearless it means you're willing to move even while questions remain.

Like Abraham, you don't need all the details to obey.
You only need the courage to align your steps with
God's voice. When your heart is aligned,
your movement becomes purposeful
and every step forward
carries divine direction.

Journaling Prompt - Inner Reflection

What familiar place, mindset, or comfort might I need to leave behind to walk in alignment?

The LORD had said to Abram, 'Go from your country, your people and your father's household to the land I will show you. - Genesis 12:1

DAY 41

Faith in Motion

Affirmation: *I take faithful steps forward, trusting God to guide each one.*

Coachable Moment:

Faith doesn't always look like giant leaps. More often, it looks like small, intentional steps taken in obedience.

We sometimes believe movement only counts if it's dramatic but God honors the step just as much as the stride. Faith in motion is choosing to act on what you know today, even when tomorrow is still unfolding.

Think of the email you've been praying about sending. The conversation you've been delaying. The quiet decision to show up differently. These small movements matter. Each step builds momentum, clarity, and confidence.

God doesn't ask you to run ahead—He invites you to walk with Him. As you move in faith, He meets you in the motion and reveals the next step at just the right time.

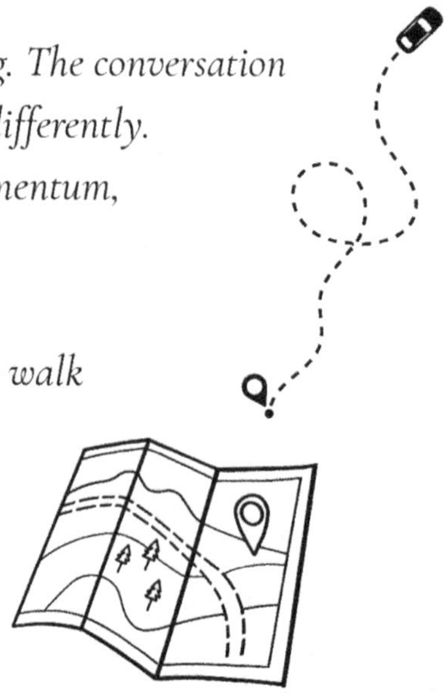

Journaling Prompt - Inner Reflection

Where might I be waiting for certainty when God is asking me to move with trust?

By faith Abraham, when called to go to a place he would later receive as his inheritance, obeyed and went, even though he did not know where he was going. - Hebrews 11:8

DAY 42

Bold Obedience

Affirmation: *I walk in bold obedience, trusting God with my steps and outcome.*

Coachable Moment:

Bold obedience is not loud.
It is settled.

It's the decision to move forward even when fear still whispers. Even when the outcome isn't guaranteed. Even when the path requires faith more than certainty.

Bold obedience grows out of trust. Trust that God sees what you cannot. Trust that He will meet you in the movement. Trust that your yes, when aligned with His direction, carries weight and purpose.

At some point, preparation turns into participation.
Vision turns into action. Faith turns into follow-through.
This is that moment.

You are not being reckless.
You are being responsive.

Today, choose bold obedience. Not because you feel fearless, but because you feel called.

Journaling Prompt - Inner Reflection

What would it look like to move forward with confidence instead of hesitation?

Blessed are those who hear the word of God and obey it. - Luke 11:28

DAY 43

Grounded After the Yes

Affirmation: *I am grounded in peace after my yes. I am standing on holy ground.*

Coachable Moment:

After a bold yes, it's natural to feel a mix of emotions. Relief. Anticipation. Maybe even uncertainty. That doesn't mean you made the wrong choice. It means you stepped into something new.

Obedience often brings a quiet moment afterward — a pause where God invites you to settle, breathe, and trust. This is not a time to replay your decision or question your courage. It's a time to remain grounded in peace.

You've done your part by responding. Now allow God to do His.
You don't need to rush the outcome or manage the results.
What's been set in motion will unfold in His timing.

Stay present. Stay anchored.
Let peace confirm what faith already decided.

Journaling Prompt - Inner Reflection

What emotions am I noticing after saying yes to God?
How can I remain grounded and present instead of overanalyzing what comes next?

....

....

....

....

....

....

....

....

....

....

....

....

You will keep in perfect peace those whose minds are steadfast, because they trust in you. - Isaiah 26:3

DAY 44

I Trust the Process

Affirmation: *I trust the God is leading me through. I cultivate remaining steady, patient, and faithful.*

Coachable Moment:

After you say yes and take the step, there is often a space in between.
The moment after obedience.
The season before visible results.

This space is not empty.
It's intentional.

God uses these moments to deepen trust, strengthen character, and remind you that the process matters just as much as the promise. You are not being delayed.
You are being developed.

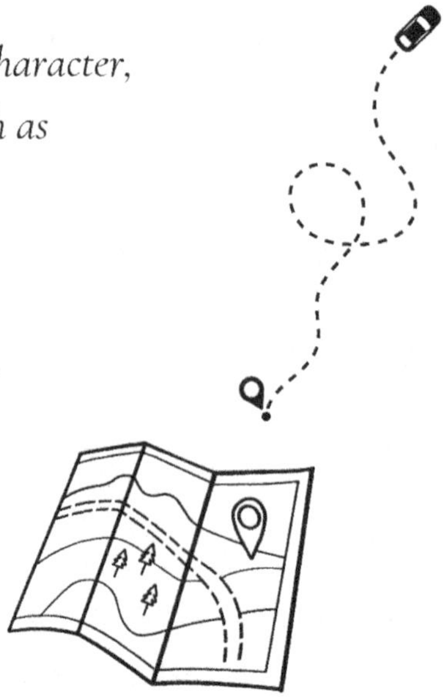

It can be tempting to rush ahead or question whether you did enough. But trust grows when you learn to stay present instead of constantly reaching for what's next.

Today, resist the urge to force movement. Stay open.
Stay faithful. Allow God to work in ways you cannot yet see.

Journaling Prompt - Inner Reflection

Where do I feel tempted to rush the process instead of trusting it?

Being confident of this, that He who began a good work in you will carry it on to completion until the day of Christ Jesus. - Philippians 1:6

DAY 45

Moving Again with Intention

Affirmation: *I move forward with intention, guided by peace.*

Coachable Moment:

There is a difference between resting and remaining still for too long.
Rest restores you.
But intention moves you forward.

After seasons of reflection and grounding, God gently invites you to engage again not with pressure, but with purpose. This isn't about rushing ahead or forcing progress. It's about responding to the quiet nudge to move.

Reactivation doesn't require a big leap. It begins with awareness. With listening. With asking, "What is the next faithful step?"

You don't need to revisit the past or second-guess your yes.
You've already laid the foundation.

Let your movement be measured.
Let your steps be intentional.

Journaling Prompt - Inner Reflection

Where do I sense God gently inviting me to engage again?

In their hearts humans plan their course, but the LORD establishes their steps. - Proverbs 16:9

DAY 46

Consistency Over Intensity

Affirmation: *I choose steady faithfulness over momentary intensity.*

Coachable Moment:

Intensity can be exciting, but it rarely lasts.

Consistency is quieter. It doesn't seek attention or instant results. It shows up day after day, doing the work that doesn't always feel dramatic — but always makes a difference.

God is not asking you for constant intensity. He's inviting you into faithfulness. The kind that builds over time. The kind that creates real change.

Small steps taken consistently will take you further than occasional bursts of effort. It's the daily decisions, the repeated habits, the quiet obedience that shape your life and your dreams.

Today, release the pressure to do everything at once.

Journaling Prompt - Inner Reflection

Where in my life have I been relying on intensity instead of consistency?

Let us not become weary in doing good, for at the proper time
we will reap a harvest if we do not give up. - Galatians 6:9

DAY 47

Building Dream Habits

Affirmation: *I build habits that strengthen the foundation of my dream, support my purpose and aligns my life with God's will.*

Coachable Moment:

Daily dream habits are not about perfection.
They're about intention.

The habits you practice daily shape the direction of your life more than the moments of inspiration you feel occasionally. What you consistently return to becomes what you rely on.

Building daily dream habits doesn't mean overhauling everything at once concerning your goals. It means choosing small, meaningful rhythms that keep you connected to God — prayer, reflection, stillness, obedience, and trust.

These habits create space for God to meet you in ordinary moments. They anchor you when motivation fades and guide you when decisions feel unclear.

Start where you are. Stay consistent.
Let faith be woven into your everyday life.

Journaling Prompt - Inner Reflection

What habits currently support my faith?
What is one daily dream habit I can begin or strengthen in this season?

....

....

....

....

....

....

....

....

....

....

....

....

But as for you be strong and do not give up, for your work will be rewarded. - 2nd Chronicles 15:7

DAY 48

Leading With Your Dream

Affirmation: *I lead with courage, and conviction. I honor the dream God placed within me by walking it out.*

Coachable Moment:

Your dream was never meant to stay private.
It was entrusted to you so it could lead you forward — and eventually, lead others too.

Leading with your dream doesn't mean you have all the answers. It means you take responsibility for what God has shown you. You move with intention. You make decisions rooted in prayer, not pressure. You allow the dream to shape how you show up, speak up, and step forward.

Leadership begins the moment you stop waiting for permission and start stewarding what's already in your hands.
When you lead with your dream, your actions align with your calling, your confidence grows, and your influence expands naturally.

You don't lead because you feel ready.
You lead because you are willing.

Today, choose to honor your dream by walking in it.

Journaling Prompt - Inner Reflection

How is my dream inviting me to lead differently in this season?

Where there is no vision, the people perish. - Proverbs 29:18

DAY 49

I Am No Longer Available for What Diminishes Me

Affirmation: *I choose environments, relationships, and habits that honor who God is shaping me to become.*

Coachable Moment:

You set the standard for how you are treated, what you accept, and what you give your energy to whether consciously or by default.

If something consistently drains your peace, dims your light, or causes you to question your worth, it deserves your discernment. Not everything that is familiar is healthy. Not everything that once fit still belongs. Growth requires release.

You are not required to justify protecting your peace.
You are not obligated to remain connected to what no longer aligns with your purpose. Outgrowing something doesn't make you disloyal—it means you're listening.

The version of you who knows her worth and stands in her God-given authority is waiting for you to choose her.

Honor the life God is building within you

Journaling Prompt - Inner Reflection

Where might God be inviting me to set a boundary, release something, or realign my priorities?

....

....

....

....

....

....

....

....

....

....

....

....

Keep your heart with all diligence, for out of it spring the issues of life. - Proverbs 4:23

HOLY PAUSE

A Sacred Moment of Rest and Reflection

DAY 50

Coachable Moment: *Chosen When Overlooked*

There are moments in life when it feels like everyone else was considered—and you were forgotten. David knew that feeling. When the prophet Samuel came to Jesse's house to anoint the next king, David wasn't even invited into the room. His own father lined up the sons he believed were most qualified, most impressive, most likely. David was left in the fields, tending sheep, unseen and overlooked.

But God's plan did not move forward without him.

"There is still one more."

David was called in—not because man
remembered him, but because God never forgot him.
Your calling and dream does not depend on
approval, or recognition by man. If God has spoken over
your life, He knows exactly where to find you!
You will not miss your divine door nor will any other man
take your assigned seat.

Journaling Prompt - Inner Reflection

Where in my life have I felt overlooked or not considered?
What truth does God want me to believe about myself today?

....

....

....

....

....

....

....

....

....

....

....

....

For the Lord does not look at the things people look at. People look at the outward appearance but the Lord looks at the heart. - 1st Samuel 16:7

DAY 51

You Were Never Meant to Carry This Alone

Affirmation: *I allow myself to receive support, rest, and connection. I am strengthened through community*

Coachable Moment:

Carrying out your God-size dream doesn't mean being isolated.

God never intended for you to carry your calling alone. Community is not a weakness — it's a gift. It's where encouragement is exchanged, burdens are shared, and strength is renewed.

After moments of affirmation and clarity, it's tempting to retreat inward or push ahead independently. But wisdom invites you to pause, connect, and rest. Even Jesus withdrew, rested, and surrounded Himself with others.

Rest is not a delay.
Connection is not a distraction.
Both are part of how God sustains you.
The journey ahead requires not just courage,
but companionship.

You don't have to prove anything.
You are allowed to be held.

Journaling Prompt - Inner Reflection

Where might God be inviting me to lean into community or connection right now?

....

....

....

....

....

....

....

....

....

....

....

....

Two are better than one..If either of them falls down,
one can help the other up. - Ecclesiastes 4:9-10

DAY 52

I Am No Longer Shrinking for Others

Affirmation: *I was created to shine. I no longer shrink to make others comfortable .*

Coachable Moment:

Your light is meant to be seen.

Too often, we downplay our gifts, mute our voices, or dim our shine to avoid making others uncomfortable. But the truth is—playing small serves no one.

Your success, confidence, and growth will inspire the right people and challenge the ones who aren't ready. Either way, that's not your burden to carry.

Step fully into your light. Own it. Shine anyway.

Journaling Prompt - Inner Reflection

Where in your life have you been shrinking? How can you show up fully and unapologetically today ?

....

....

....

....

....

....

....

....

....

....

....

....

No one lights a lamp and then puts it under a basket. Instead, a lamp is placed on a stand, where it gives light to everyone in the house. - Matthew 5:15

DAY 53

I Am Walking in My Authority

Affirmation: *I am powerful, anointed, and fully equipped for my purpose. I walk in my authority*

Coachable Moment:

You were not created to live in doubt, hesitation, or fear. You were created to stand in your power and move with confidence.

When you second-guess yourself, you disconnect from the God-given truth of your identity and the position you hold as His who is deeply loved. You are already enough. You don't need more credentials, more approval, or more perfection. God has already qualified you.

Stop questioning your power. Own it. Walk in it. Lead with it.

Journaling Prompt - Inner Reflection

Where in your life have you been shrinking instead of standing in your authority? How can you reclaim your power today?

Wait for the LORD; be strong and take heart and wait for the LORD. - Psalm 27:14

DAY 54

I Am Unstoppable

Affirmation: *Nothing can block what God has for me. I am focused, fearless, and unstoppable.*

Coachable Moment:

Obstacles don't mean stop—they mean keep going.

Every setback, delay, and closed door is a test: Will you quit, or will you push through? The difference between those who succeed and those who don't isn't talent—it's resilience.
You are stronger than the challenges in front of you. You will not break. You will not back down. You are UNSTOPPABLE.

Journaling Prompt - Inner Reflection

What is one challenge you are currently facing?
How can you shift your mindset and move forward with unstoppable force?

....

....

....

....

....

....

....

....

....

....

....

....

You have given me your shield of victory. Your right hand supports me;
your help has made me great. - Psalm 18:135

DAY 55

I Am Walking in Divine Timing

Affirmation: *Everything is unfolding exactly as it should. I trust God's perfect timing for my life."*

Coachable Moment:

You are not behind. You are exactly where you need to be.
Comparison will have you thinking you're late, but God is never in a rush.
What's meant for you will not pass you by. The delay isn't a denial—it's divine preparation.

Rest in the knowing that when it's time, IT WILL HAPPEN

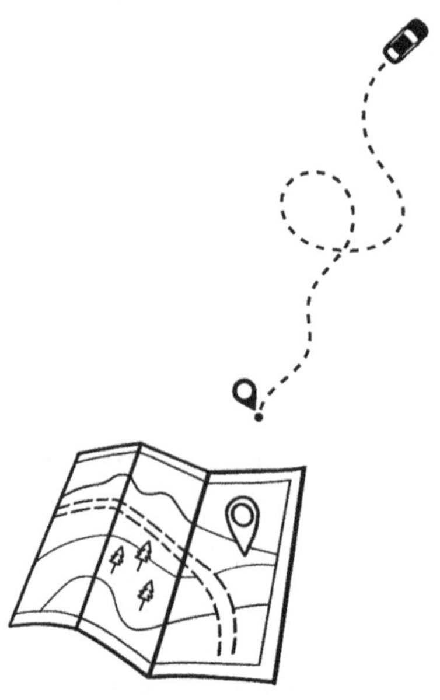

Journaling Prompt - Inner Reflection

In this season of your life how can you maintain your personal pace?

The LORD will work out His plans for my life for your faithful love,
O LORD endures forever. - Psalm 138:8

DAY 56

I Am Fearless in Pursuit of My Calling

Affirmation: *I refuse to let fear stop me. I move forward boldly in my purpose.*

Coachable Moment:

Fear is a liar. It will tell you that you're not ready, that you'll fail, that you don't have what it takes. But none of that is true.

Fear only has power when you let it stop you. What if you did it scared? What if you moved forward anyway?

Courage isn't about never feeling fear—it's about refusing to let it hold you back. Your purpose is bigger than your fear. Move. Now.

Journaling Prompt - Inner Reflection

What is one fear that's been keeping you stuck? What action can you take today to move forward despite it?

Don't be afraid, for I am with you. Don't be discouraged, for I am your God. I will strengthen you and help you. - Isaiah 41:10

DAY 57

I Am Aligned with My Assignment

Affirmation: *I am in divine alignment. My steps are guided, and my purpose is clear*

Coachable Moment:

There's a difference between being busy and being aligned. When you're aligned, there's flow, clarity, and peace—even in the hard work.

You don't have to force what's meant for you. When you're aligned with your assignment, doors open, ideas flow, and peace follows.

Today, check in with yourself. Are you moving with purpose and intention or just creating a lot of commotion? Clarity lives in alignment.

Journaling Prompt - Inner Reflection

Where in your life do you feel most aligned? What shifts can you make to move deeper into your purpose?

The LORD replied, My Presence will go with you,
and I will give you rest. - Exodus 33:14

DAY 58

I Am Rooted, Not Rushed

Affirmation: *I do not chase. I prepare, align, and attract. I am rooted in purpose, not rushed by pressure.*

Coachable Moment:

The pressure to "hurry up and make it" can feel overwhelming. But rushing leads to burnout, not breakthrough.

A tree doesn't grow overnight—it takes deep roots before it ever bears fruit. The same is true for you.

Stay rooted in faith. Rooted in vision. Rooted in who you're becoming. You don't have to prove anything to anyone. Let God grow you in His timing.

Journaling Prompt - Inner Reflection

Where have you been rushing or forcing things in your life? What would it look like to slow down and trust your growth process?

That person is like a tree planted by streams of water, which yield its fruit in season and whose leaf does not wither-whatever they do prospers. - Psalm 1:3

DAY 59

I Am Becoming Who I Prayed For

Affirmation: *I am walking in answered prayers. I honor the woman I'm becoming.*

Coachable Moment:

Take a moment—look around. Some of the things you have today are the very things you once prayed for.

It's easy to keep reaching for the next goal, but don't miss the beauty of what you've already stepped into. Growth is happening. Transformation is unfolding.

You are becoming her—the woman you dreamed of, the woman you prayed to be. Keep going, she's proud of you.

Journaling Prompt - Inner Reflection

As you pause take a moment to reflect. What answered prayers are you standing in right now. Let's celebrate the Faithfulness of God!

That person is like a tree planted by streams of water, which yield its fruit in season and whose leaf does not wither-whatever they do prospers. - Psalm 1:3

HOLY PAUSE

A Sacred Moment of Rest and Reflection

DAY 60

Coachable Moment: *Strength in the Waiting*

Hannah's strength was not loud—but it was unwavering.

She carried a longing that felt heavy and unseen. Year after year, she prayed. She wept. She returned to God again and again with the same request, trusting Him even when the waiting stretched longer than she expected.

Hannah teaches us that waiting does not mean weakness. Persistence in prayer is not desperation—it is faith that refuses to let go of hope. Even when her circumstances did not change immediately, her posture remained rooted in trust.

This Holy Pause is a reminder that emotional fatigue can creep in when answers feel delayed. But prayer is not a last resort—it is a lifeline. In the waiting, God is still listening. He is still working. And He is still faithful to His timing.

If you find yourself weary today, know this: unseen faith is still powerful faith.

Journaling Prompt - Inner Reflection

Where have you been praying faithfully, yet waiting longer than you expected? What would it look like to trust God with both your longing and His timing?

Don't think I am a wicked woman! For I have been praying out of great anguish and sorrow. - 1st Samuel 1:16

DAY 61

I Am Enough Even While Becoming

Affirmation: *I am a work in progress and still fully worthy. I am enough in every version of me."*

Coachable Moment:

You don't have to wait until you've "arrived" to be worthy. You are enough now—in the messy middle, in the healing, in the rebuilding.

Becoming doesn't mean broken. You can hold grace and growth at the same time. You don't need to earn your worth—it's already within you.

Keep becoming. But don't forget: you're already enough.

Journaling Prompt - Inner Reflection

What part of your journey do you tend to judge or minimize? How can you offer yourself more grace and acceptance today?

The fastest runner doesn't always win the race, and the strongest warrior doesn't always win the battle. - Ecclesiastes 9:11

DAY 62

I Release the Need to Control Everything

Affirmation: *I trust in divine guidance. I surrender and allow life to unfold in perfect timing.*

Coachable Moment:

Trying to control every detail only leads to exhaustion and frustration. Peace lives in surrender. You don't have to have it all figured out—you just have to trust the One who does.

Let go. Release the grip. Your job is to show up; God's job is to lead the way.

Journaling Prompt - Inner Reflection

Where in your life are you trying to control the outcome?
How can you practice surrender today?

The fastest runner doesn't always win the race, and the strongest warrior doesn't always win the battle. - Ecclesiastes 9:11

DAY 63

God's Plans Are Greater Than Mine

Affirmation: *I surrender my timeline. I trust that what's coming is better than what I imagined.*

Coachable Moment:

It's hard when things don't go the way you hoped—but sometimes the "no" is actually a redirection to something better.

You might not see it yet, but God's plan is never to harm—it's always to grow, guide, and elevate you. What feels like delay is often divine protection.

Trust the reroute.
Trust His heart.

Journaling Prompt - Inner Reflection

What outcome have you been holding tightly to? How can you practice surrender and believe that something greater is unfolding?

....

....

....

....

....

....

....

....

....

....

....

....

No eye has seen, no ear has heard, and no mind has imagined
what God has prepared for those who love him. - 1st Corinthians 2:9

DAY 64

Gratitude Changes Everything

Affirmation: *I choose to focus on my blessings. Gratitude shifts my heart and my perspective.*

Coachable Moment:

Gratitude is a lens—it doesn't change your circumstances, but it changes how you see them.

When you choose to see through the eyes of gratitude, peace multiplies. Joy expands. Frustration fades. What you focus on, grows—so let your focus be on the good.

Journaling Prompt - Inner Reflection

What are three things you're grateful for today—big or small? How does naming them shift your energy?

The LORD is my strength and shield; in him my heart trusts, and I am helped;
my heart exults, and with my song I give thanks to him. - Psalm 28:7

DAY 65

I Make Room for More

Affirmation: *I create space for abundance. I release what no longer serves me.*

Coachable Moment:

Overflow can't pour into clutter. Whether it's your mindset, your habits, or your environment—some things may need to be released to receive the new.

Making room for more means trusting that what's leaving is making space for something greater. Open hands. Open heart. Open future.

Journaling Prompt - Inner Reflection

What do you need to release to make room for what's next? How will letting go create space for growth?

....

....

....

....

....

....

....

....

....

....

....

....

The LORD will the open heavens, the storehouse of his bounty, to send rain on your land in season and to bless all the work of your hands. - Deuteronomy 28:12

DAY 66

The Best is Yet to Come

Affirmation: *My future is bright. I believe in what's ahead, even when I can't see it yet.*

Coachable Moment:

This isn't the end of your story—it's just the beginning. You've made it through so much, and God is not finished with you yet.

Hold onto hope. Expect good things. Speak life over your future. You've come too far not to believe that the best is still unfolding for you.

Journaling Prompt - Inner Reflection

What would it look like to truly believe that the best is yet to come?
What are you most hopeful for right now?

Now to him who is able to do immeasurable more than all we ask or imagine,
according to his power that is at work within you. - Ephesians 3:20

DAY 67

An Overcomer by Design

Affirmation: *I am an overcomer through Christ. My story, my testimony, and my faith carry power. Nothing I have walked through was wasted.*

Coachable Moment:

You are not an overcomer because life was easy.
You are an overcomer because you endured, learned, rose, and kept believing—even when it hurt.

Your testimony is not just about the victories you celebrate—it includes the failures you survived, the pain you healed from, the doubts you wrestled with, and the courage it took to keep going. Every season shaped you. Every hurdle strengthened you. Every win reminded you of God's faithfulness.

The enemy wants you silent—ashamed of your past, minimizing your growth, questioning your worth. But God invites you to remember: what you've walked through is evidence of His power at work within you.

Your story matters.
Not because it's perfect—but because it's real.
And when you own it, speak it, and honor it,
you break chains not only for yourself, but for others who need hope.

Journaling Prompt - Inner Reflection

What experiences in my life has God used to shape, strengthen, or refine me? How can I honor my story instead of hiding it?

....

....

....

....

....

....

....

....

....

....

....

....

And they overcame him by the blood of the Lamb , and the word of their testimony. - Revelations 12:11

DAY 68

My Life Is a Reflection of God's Goodness

Affirmation: *I walk in gratitude. Every part of my journey carries purpose and grace.*

Coachable Moment:

Even the quiet seasons. Even the detours. Even the delays.
God's hand has been in it all. Actively moving and working on your behalf.

When you take a step back, you'll begin to see the thread of His goodness weaving everything together. The fact that you're still here is evidence enough

Journaling Prompt - Inner Reflection

Where have you seen God's goodness show up in unexpected ways?

But the LORD is faithful, He will establish you and guard against the evil one. - 2nd Thessalonians 3:3

DAY 69

Rising With Purpose

Affirmation: *I rise in faith, courage, and obedience. I step fully into who God has called me to be.*

Coachable Moment:

There comes a moment when waiting turns into arising.

"Rising" is not a suggestion—it is a divine invitation. It is the call to stand up from hesitation, to shake off fear, and to move forward with holy confidence. You don't arise because you feel ready; you arise because God has called you.

Rising doesn't mean everything is clear. It means you trust God enough to move before clarity "fully" comes. It means choosing obedience over comfort and faith over familiarity.

You are not rising in your own strength—you are rising in God's power. The same God who called you is the same God who will sustain you. What once felt heavy no longer has permission to hold you down.

This is your moment to rise—not later, not someday, not when conditions are perfect but now.

Journaling Prompt - Inner Reflection

Where in my life is God inviting me to rise?
What fears, doubts, or excuses do I need to release?

Arise, shine, for your light has come, and the glory of the Lord is upon you.
- Isaiah 60:1

HOLY PAUSE

A Sacred Moment of Rest and Reflection

DAY 70

Coachable Moment: *Steady in the Rise*

Joseph's life reminds us that rising does not happen overnight—it happens through faithfulness in every season.

He was given a dream, but before the fulfillment came the pit, the prison, and years of waiting. Yet Joseph did not abandon integrity while waiting for elevation. He remained steady—trusting God's process even when the promise felt distant. What's powerful about Joseph's story is not just that he rose, but how he rose. God had a set time for restoration. Regardless of the many life events that appeared to be detours or delays God's plan and vision for his life was fulfilled. He didn't grow bitter in obscurity. He stayed grounded in who God had called him to be, even when circumstances suggested otherwise.

This Holy Pause invites you to remember: rising with purpose requires steadiness. God is not only interested in lifting you—He is committed to forming you. The same faith that carried you through hidden seasons will sustain you as you rise.

Journaling Prompt - Inner Reflection

Where in my life is God asking me to remain steady while I rise?

....

....

....

....

....

....

....

....

....

....

....

....

You intended to harm me, but God intended if for good to accomplish what is now being done, the saving of many lives.

- Genesis 50:20

DAY 71

Prayer Is a Lifeline

Affirmation: *Prayer anchors me, strengthens me, and keeps me connected to the dream God has placed within me.*

Coachable Moment:

Every dream needs a lifeline—and prayer is yours.

Prayer is not a last resort; it is the sustaining force that keeps your dream alive. When clarity feels distant, when strength feels low, when the journey feels heavier than expected, prayer becomes the place where you are renewed, realigned, and reminded of why you began.

Through prayer, you release what you were never meant to carry alone. You receive wisdom, peace, and direction for each step ahead. Prayer keeps your heart soft, your spirit attentive, and your focus anchored on God rather than the obstacles around you.

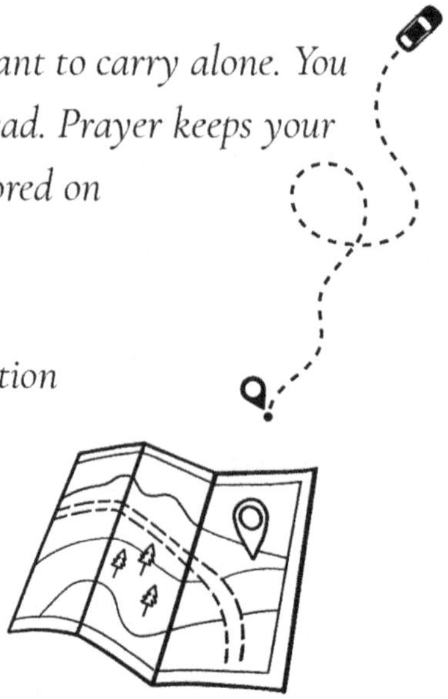

Dreams are sustained in the quiet moments of connection—when no one is watching, when answers haven't come yet, and when faith must rise before results appear. Prayer keeps the vision breathing while God does the work you cannot see.

Journaling Prompt - Inner Reflection

Where have you seen God's goodness show up in unexpected ways?

....

....

....

....

....

....

....

....

....

....

....

....

But the LORD is faithful, He will establish you and guard against the evil one. - 2nd Thessalonians 3:3

DAY 72

Walking in the Light of the Word

Affirmation: *God's Word guides my steps and brings clarity to my path. I move forward with wisdom and trust.*

Coachable Moment:

There are seasons when God does not reveal the entire path—only the next step.

That is where His Word becomes essential. The Word of God does not always light the whole road ahead, but it faithfully illuminates what you need to see right now. It keeps you grounded, focused, and moving in the right direction even when the journey feels uncertain.

You don't need complete clarity to move forward. You need obedience to what has already been revealed. God's Word anchors your decisions, steadies your heart, and guards you from walking by fear or emotion alone.

When you stay close to the Word,
you stay aligned with truth. It reminds
you who God is, who you are,
and where you are going.

Journaling Prompt - Inner Reflection

Where do I need God's guidance for my next step rather than the full picture? How can I intentionally stay rooted in God's Word during this season?

Your word is a lamp for my feet, a light on my path. - Psalm 119:105

DAY 73

Guided by the Holy Spirit

Affirmation: *The Holy Spirit leads me with wisdom and clarity. I trust His guidance, even when the route changes.*

Coachable Moment:

Think about how a GPS works in your car.

It doesn't show you the entire journey—only the next turn. It recalculates when you miss an exit or encounter a delay. It doesn't shame you for wrong turns; it simply keeps guiding you forward. The Holy Spirit leads in much the same way.

He doesn't overwhelm you with every detail of your future. Instead, He guides you moment by moment—prompting, correcting, and reassuring you as you move. When you pause, hesitate, or misstep, He doesn't abandon you. He redirects you. The key is staying connected. The Holy Spirit aligns your steps and keeps you moving toward God's purpose.
You don't have to fear getting lost.
You are never navigating alone.

Trust the guidance. Follow the prompting.
The Holy Spirit is your faithful companion.

Journaling Prompt - Inner Reflection

How can I become more attentive to the Holy Spirit's guidance today?

But when he, the Spirit of truth, comes, he will guide you into all truth. - John 16:13

DAY 74

I Am Focused, Not Distracted

Affirmation: *I am focused, grounded, and discerning as I move forward. I guard what God is growing in me.*

Coachable Moment:

Focus is not something you find—it's something you choose and protect.

As you continue moving forward, staying focused matters more than ever. Not because you're doing something wrong, but because progress often attracts subtle distractions meant to pull your attention off course.

Distraction shifts your attention away from what God has entrusted to you. It may seem harmless, but over time it can dilute your energy and clarity.

Discouragement often shows up quietly—when results take longer than expected or the journey feels heavier than imagined. If left unchecked, it can cause you to question what God has already confirmed.

Derailment happens when small compromises go unnoticed, slowly moving you off alignment.

Choosing focus doesn't require striving—it requires awareness. When you stay connected, you remain steady and aligned.

Journaling Prompt - Inner Reflection

Which of the three D's-distraction, discouragement, or derailment do I need to be most aware of right now?

Those who live in the shelter of the Most High will find rest in the shadow of the Almighty. - Psalm 91:1

DAY 75

I Trust the Season I'm In

Affirmation: *I release the need to rush. My journey is unfolding in divine timing.*

Coachable Moment:

There is nothing missing. You are not late. You're not behind. This moment matters just as much as the destination.

Breathe. Trust God. Keep showing up and tending to the soil of your dream and vision. Everything is coming together—just as it should.

Journaling Prompt - Inner Reflection

What makes you feel like you "should be further by now?
How can you practice trusting the timing of your life today?

Wait for it; it will surely come. - Habakkuk 2:3

DAY 76

I Speak Life Over My Future

Affirmation: *I release the need to rush. My journey is unfolding in divine timing.*

Coachable Moment:

There is nothing missing. You are not late. You're not behind. This moment matters just as much as the destination.

Breathe. Trust God. Keep showing up and tending to the soil of your dream and vision. Everything is coming together—just as it should.

Journaling Prompt - Inner Reflection

What makes you feel like you "should be further by now?
How can you practice trusting the timing of your life today?

Wait for it; it will surely come. - Habakkuk 2:3

DAY 77

God's Promises Never Fail

Affirmation: *I hold onto faith. What God said, He will do.*

Coachable Moment:

When doubt creeps in, go back to what God promised. He's not a man that He should lie. His timing may stretch you, but His word will never fail you.

Even in silence, He's still working. Even in waiting, He's still faithful. Stand on His promises—they're your foundation.

Journaling Prompt - Inner Reflection

What promise from God do you need to revisit and stand on today?

....

....

....

....

....

....

....

....

....

....

....

....

God is not a man, he does not lie. He is not human, so he does not change his mind.
Has he ever spoken and failed to act? Has he ever promised and not carried it through so- Habakkuk 2:3

DAY 78

I Am Walking Into My Winning Season

Affirmation: *I believe in what's coming. This is my season of overflow and elevation.*

Coachable Moment:

You've sowed the seeds. You've weathered the storm. Now, it's harvest time.

This season is not random—it's the result of your faith, growth, obedience, and perseverance. Don't downplay it. Don't second-guess it. You're stepping into everything you've been preparing for.

Journaling Prompt - Inner Reflection

What does your "winning season" look and feel like?
How can you show up like you're already in it?

They that sow in tears shall reap with joy. - Psalm 126

DAY 79

Not Every Voice Is Meant to Guide Me

Affirmation: *I listen with wisdom and discernment. I honor counsel, but I follow God's leading above all else.*

Coachable Moment:

As you grow, your circle of voices will naturally increase—but not every voice deserves authority in your life.

Expansion brings attention, opinions, and advice from many directions. Some voices are well-meaning. Others are rooted in fear, comparison, or their own limitations. Discernment is learning the difference between feedback that sharpens you and noise that distracts you. Wisdom doesn't require isolation, but it does require intentional listening.

God often speaks through trusted counsel, Scripture, and quiet conviction—not through pressure, confusion, or urgency.
The voices you give access to your heart will influence how you move, when you act, and what you believe about yourself.

In this season you *are not obligated to carry every opinion or respond to every voice.*
You are invited to remain attentive to God's guidance and anchored in truth.

Choose wisely who you listen to. Your growth depends on it.

Journaling Prompt - Inner Reflection

Whose voices have I been giving weight to in this season?
How can I create more space to listen for God's direction above all else?

My sheep listen to my voice; I know them, and they follow me. - John 10:27

HOLY PAUSE

A Sacred Moment of Rest and Reflection

DAY 80

Coachable Moment: *For Such a Time as This*

Esther's story reminds us that purpose often unfolds quietly before it ever becomes visible. She didn't rush into her calling. She listened. She waited. She sought wisdom.

Before she spoke publicly, she was formed privately. Before she acted boldly, she paused to discern the moment. Esther understood something powerful: timing matters. Courage is not reckless—it is obedient. And influence is not seized; it is stewarded.

There were many voices around her, but she learned which ones to trust. There were real risks involved, but she didn't move until she was aligned. When the moment came, she stepped forward—not driven by fear, but grounded in purpose. This Holy Pause is an invitation to recognize where God has positioned you. You are not here by accident. The season you're in, the influence you carry, and the opportunities before you are part of a divine design.

Rest here. Reflect. Listen.

Journaling Prompt - Inner Reflection

Where do I sense God has positioned me for this season? What wisdom, discernment, or courage might God be inviting me to lean into right now?

And who knows but that you have come to your royal position
for such a time as this? - Esther 4:14

DAY 81

Step Forward With Courage

Affirmation: *I move forward with courage and trust. God is with me in every step I take.*

Coachable Moment:

After moments of rest and reflection, there comes a time to move.

Courage doesn't always look bold or loud. Often, it looks like taking the next step even when your voice shakes, your heart beats faster, or the outcome remains uncertain. It's choosing obedience over comfort and trust over fear.

Like Esther, there may be moments when stepping forward feels costly. But courage rooted in faith is never reckless—it is intentional, prayerful, and aligned. You don't need to know how everything will unfold. You only need to be willing to move when God says, now.

Today is not about doing everything. It's about doing the one thing God is inviting you to do next. When you move in courage, God meets you with grace, clarity, and strength.

Step forward. You are not alone.

Journaling Prompt - Inner Reflection

What step is God inviting me to take in this season? What fears do I need to surrender so I can move forward with courage?

Have I not commanded you? Be strong and courageous. Do not be afraid, do not be discouraged, for the LORD your God will be with you wherever you go. - Joshua 1:9

DAY 82

My Gifts Will Make Room for Me

Affirmation: *I honor and steward the gifts God placed within me. I boldly share what He has entrusted to me and allow it to serve others.*

Coachable Moment:

God did not place gifts inside of you for them to remain hidden. Your skills, ideas, creativity, and calling were designed to be seen, used, and shared.

Making room for your gift means giving it space to grow, develop, and reach the people it was meant to serve. There is nothing unspiritual about letting others know what you offer. Sharing your work, promoting your business, and highlighting your abilities are part of stewardship—not pride. When your heart is aligned, visibility becomes service.

Your gift carries purpose beyond you. When you show up confidently and speak clearly about what you do, you create access for others to be helped, inspired, and impacted. God uses willing vessels who are unafraid to be seen.

Don't shrink back. Don't downplay what He has given you. Make room for your gift to breathe, expand, and do what it was created to do.

Remember when God gives a gift, He also gives grace for placement.

Journaling Prompt - Inner Reflection

What gifts has God placed within me that I'm learning to steward faithfully?

A gift opens the way and ushers the giver into the presence of the great. - Joshua 1:9

DAY 83

Lead With What You Carry

Affirmation: *I lead with confidence, wisdom, and purpose. What God has placed within me is meant to influence and serve.*

Coachable Moment:

Leadership doesn't always come with a title—it often begins with a response.

You lead when you answer the call of your dream. When you say yes to what God has placed on your heart, even before you feel fully ready, you step into leadership. Obedience is often the first expression of leadership.

You lead when you take responsibility for what you carry. When you steward your gifts, show up consistently, and move with intention, your life becomes an example others can follow.

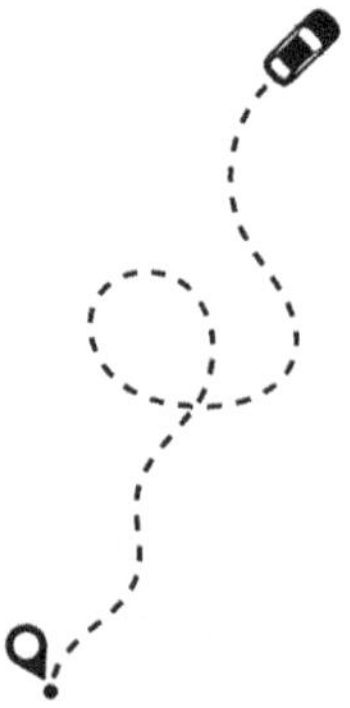

Leadership is not about having everything figured out. It's about being willing to move forward with faith, integrity, and courage. God develops leaders in motion—through choices, consistency, and trust.

You don't have to wait for permission to lead. By answering the call of your dream, you are already doing it.

Journaling Prompt - Inner Reflection

How have I already been leading by answering the call of my dream?
Where is God inviting me to take greater ownership of what I carry?

Whoever can be trusted with very little can also be trusted with much. - Luke 16:10

DAY 84

I Am a Light to Others

Affirmation: *I steward my influence with humility and intention. My life reflects truth, integrity, and hope.*

Coachable Moment:

Your life carries weight—not because you are trying to be seen, but because you are choosing to walk faithfully.

As you grow, your consistency matters more than your visibility. The way you live, respond, and remain grounded speaks louder than any title or platform. Influence isn't about performing for others; it's about stewarding who you are becoming in every season.

Don't underestimate the quiet power of integrity. As you continue to rise, let your character lead the way. A steady light doesn't flicker—it endures.

Journaling Prompt - Inner Reflection

How am I stewarding the influence God has already entrusted to me? What does it look like for me to walk consistently and faithfully in this season?

....

....

....

....

....

....

....

....

....

....

....

....

The path of the righteous is like the morning sun, shining ever brighter
til the full light of day. - Proverbs 4:18

DAY 85

Built to Last

Affirmation: *I build with patience and purpose. What God is doing in me is meant to endure.*

Coachable Moment:

This journey was never meant to be rushed.

God is not only interested in what you start — He cares deeply about what you sustain. Dreams that last are built slowly, intentionally, and with care. They are supported by strong foundations, healthy rhythms, and obedience over time.

There may be moments when you feel the urge to move faster, do more, or prove something. But longevity requires restraint as much as courage. It's not about how quickly you can move — it's about how faithfully you can remain.

You are not building for applause or a momentary win. You are building a life, a calling, and a legacy that can withstand seasons of growth, challenge, and change.

Slow down enough to build well. What God is establishing in you is meant to last.

Journaling Prompt - Inner Reflection

Where might I need to shift from rushing to building with intention? What habits or rhythms will help me sustain what God is growing in my life?

Therefore everyone who hears these words of mine and puts them into practice is like a wise man who built his house upon a rock. - Matthew 7:24-25

DAY 86

Walking in Confidence

Affirmation: *I walk with confidence rooted in truth, not validation. I am secure in who God has called me to be.*

Coachable Moment:

Confidence doesn't always announce itself.

As you grow, you may notice that you no longer feel the need to explain, defend, or prove yourself. That's not complacency — that's maturity. Quiet confidence is the fruit of walking with God long enough to trust who He has shaped you to be.

This kind of confidence isn't loud or attention-seeking. It's steady. It comes from knowing your values, honoring your process, and remaining anchored when opinions shift or expectations change.

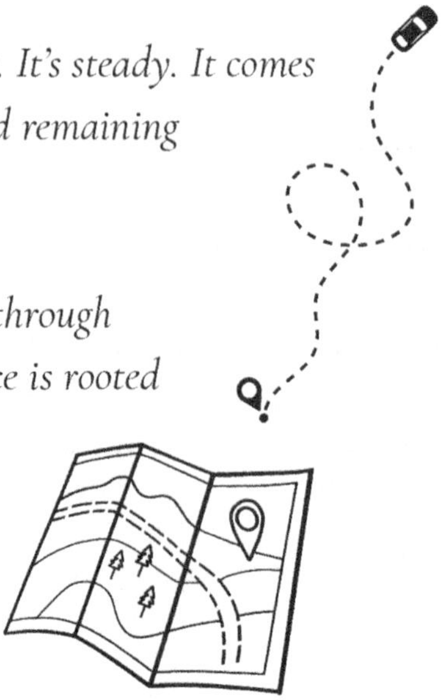

You don't need to perform to be seen. Your life speaks through consistency, integrity, and obedience. When confidence is rooted in identity rather than approval, it creates peace instead of pressure.

Walk forward today without striving.
You are secure. You are grounded. And you are becoming exactly who you were created to be.

Journaling Prompt - Inner Reflection

Where have I noticed a shift from seeking validation to walking in confidence? What helps me stay grounded in my identity when outside voices get loud?

So do not throw away your confidence; it will be richly rewarded. - Hebrews 10:35

DAY 87

Legacy Is Formed Daily

Affirmation: *I live with intention and faithfulness each day. My everyday choices are shaping a lasting legacy.*

Coachable Moment:

Legacy isn't something you leave behind one day—it's something you live out daily.

It's easy to think legacy is tied to big milestones, titles, or accomplishments. But more often, it's formed in the quiet, ordinary moments: how you show up when no one is watching, the values you live by, and the consistency you choose even when progress feels slow.

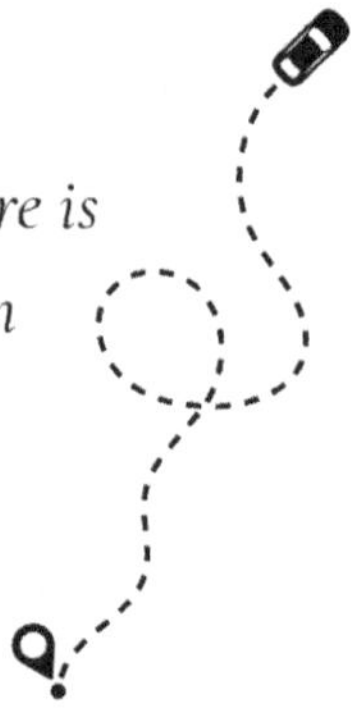

Every decision matters. The way you love, lead, forgive, and persevere is shaping the story your life tells. You don't have to wait for a platform or a future moment to begin living with purpose. You are already doing it—right here, right now.

Be present in today. Faithfulness in the small things creates impact that lasts far beyond what you can see.

Journaling Prompt - Inner Reflection

What daily habits or choices am I making that reflect the legacy I want to leave?

So Let us not become weary in doing good, for at the proper time we will reap a harvest if we do not give up. - Galatians 6:9

DAY 88

Passing It Forward

Affirmation: *I am a might oak tree planted in the house of the Lord. My life is a blessing to others.*

Coachable Moment:

Growth was never meant to stop with you.

As you've walked this journey, you've gained wisdom, perspective, and strength — not just for yourself, but so others might benefit from what you've learned. Passing it forward doesn't always look like teaching or leading formally. Sometimes it's a word of encouragement, a shared experience, or simply making space for someone else to rise.

You don't need to have everything figured out to be a blessing. Your willingness to share honestly — your lessons, your faith, your journey — can become a lifeline for someone else who is just beginning.

Generosity isn't about giving from emptiness; it flows from a heart that recognizes how much it has already received. As you continue forward, let your life be open-handed. What God has done in you can now flow through you.

Journaling Prompt - Inner Reflection

Who might God be inviting me to encourage, support, or uplift in this season? What wisdom or experience can I share that could help someone else move forward?

So Let us not become weary in doing good, for at the proper time we will reap a harvest if we do not give up. - Galatians 6:9

DAY89

Finishing Strong

Affirmation: *I finish what God has called me to with faith, endurance, and grace. I do not quit—I continue forward*

Coachable Moment:

Finishing strong doesn't mean finishing perfectly.

It means staying faithful when the journey feels long. It means continuing forward even when motivation fluctuates or progress feels unseen. Strength is not proven by how fast you move, but by your willingness to keep going.

You've grown. You've endured. You've learned to trust God not just at the starting line, but in the middle—and now, near the end of this stretch. That matters.

Don't underestimate the power of perseverance. Every step you've taken, every yes you've given, every moment you chose faith over fear has shaped who you are becoming.

Finish this season with gratitude. Carry forward what you've learned. God honors endurance, and He completes what He begins.

Journaling Prompt - Inner Reflection

What has this journey taught me about perseverance and trust? Where do I sense God inviting me to remain faithful as I move forward?

Being confident of this, that He who began a good work in you will carry it on to completion until the day of Christ Jesus. - Philippians 1:6

DAY90

She Went From Dreaming to Doing

Affirmation: *I am walking in obedience, courage, and purpose. I am becoming and I am doing.*

Coachable Moment:

This is not the end of your journey. It's the beginning of living everything you've been preparing for. You didn't just read these pages—you allowed yourself to be shaped by them. You faced doubt. You learned to trust God's timing. You guarded your focus, stewarded your gifts, and chose faith again and again. Somewhere along the way, something shifted. You did too.

Dreaming was never the destination. Obedience was. Action was. Alignment was. You may not have all the answers, and you don't need them. What you have is clarity, courage, and a deeper trust in God—and that's more than enough to move forward. So now, you go. You show up. You build. You speak. You live fully.

This journey continues beyond these pages. Carry what you've learned. Hold fast to the One who called you. Champion, steward your dream well.

She went from dreaming to doing.
And now... so will you.

Journaling Prompt - Inner Reflection

How have I changed over the course of this journey? What is God inviting me to do next as I continue walking in purpose?

....

....

....

....

....

....

....

....

....

....

....

....

Being confident of this, that He who began a good work in you will carry it on to completion until the day of Christ Jesus. - Philippians 1:6

Made in the USA
Coppell, TX
19 January 2026